FIND OUT MORE

BOOKS
Levy, Joel. *Turn It Up! A Pitch-Perfect History of Music That Rocked the World*. Washington, DC: National Geographic Kids, 2019.

Richards, Mary, and David Schweitzer. *A History of Music for Children*. London, UK: Thames & Hudson, 2021.

Trusty, Kathy. *The Story of Ella Fitzgerald*. Emeryville, CA: Rockridge Press, 2021.

WEBSITES
Explore these online sources with an adult:

Britannica Kids: Ella Fitzgerald

Children's Museum, Indianapolis: Ella Fitzgerald

Rice University: Ella Fitzgerald

INDEX

albums, 4, 18
Apollo Theater, 10–11, 13–15
Armstrong, Louis, 8, 18
bebop, 16
Boswell Sisters, 8–9, 13
Brown, Ray, 18
Carter, Benny, 15
Ellington, Duke, 18
Fitzgerald, Ella
  awards, 4, 21
  childhood, 6–13
  death, 20
  father, 6
  friendships, 10, 13, 15, 19

husband and children, 18, 20
mother, 6, 9
school, 6, 10, 12
songs, 4, 16–18, 22
Grammy Awards, 4, 21
Harlem, New York, 10–11, 14
jazz, 4–5, 8, 16–17
Newport News, Virginia, 6
racism, 19
scatting, 16
Tiny Bradshaw Band, 14
Webb, Chick, 14, 17
Yonkers, New York, 6–7

ABOUT THE AUTHOR

Joyce Markovics has written hundreds of books for kids. She appreciates the power of music to move and unite us. Joyce is grateful to all people who have beaten the odds to tell their stories and make great art. She would like to thank the wonderful Tad Hershorn, one of Ella's biggest fans, for his thoughtful contribution to this book.

GLOSSARY

amateur (AM-uh-chur) a person who is not a professional

autograph (AW-tuh-graf) a signature, especially from a famous person

chauffeur (SHOH-fer) a person whose job is to drive another person's car

devastated (DEV-uh-stay-tid) shocked or upset

feat (FEET) an act or achievement that takes courage, skill, or strength

laundromat (LAWN-druh-mat) a place that has washing machines and dryers for public use

mourned (MORND) felt very sad about someone who died

NAACP (EN-DUHB-UHL-AY-SEE-PEE) an organization set up in 1909 to fight for the rights of Black people; stands for the National Association for the Advancement of Colored People

precision (pri-SIZH-uhn) the quality of being exact and accurate

producer (pruh-DOOSS-ur) the person who is in charge of making a musical recording and helping shape the overall sound

racism (REY-siz-uhm) a system of beliefs and policies based on the idea that one race or group of people is better than another

reform school (ri-FAWRM skool) a place where young people are sent as an alternative to prison

vocal (VOH-kuhl) relating to the human voice

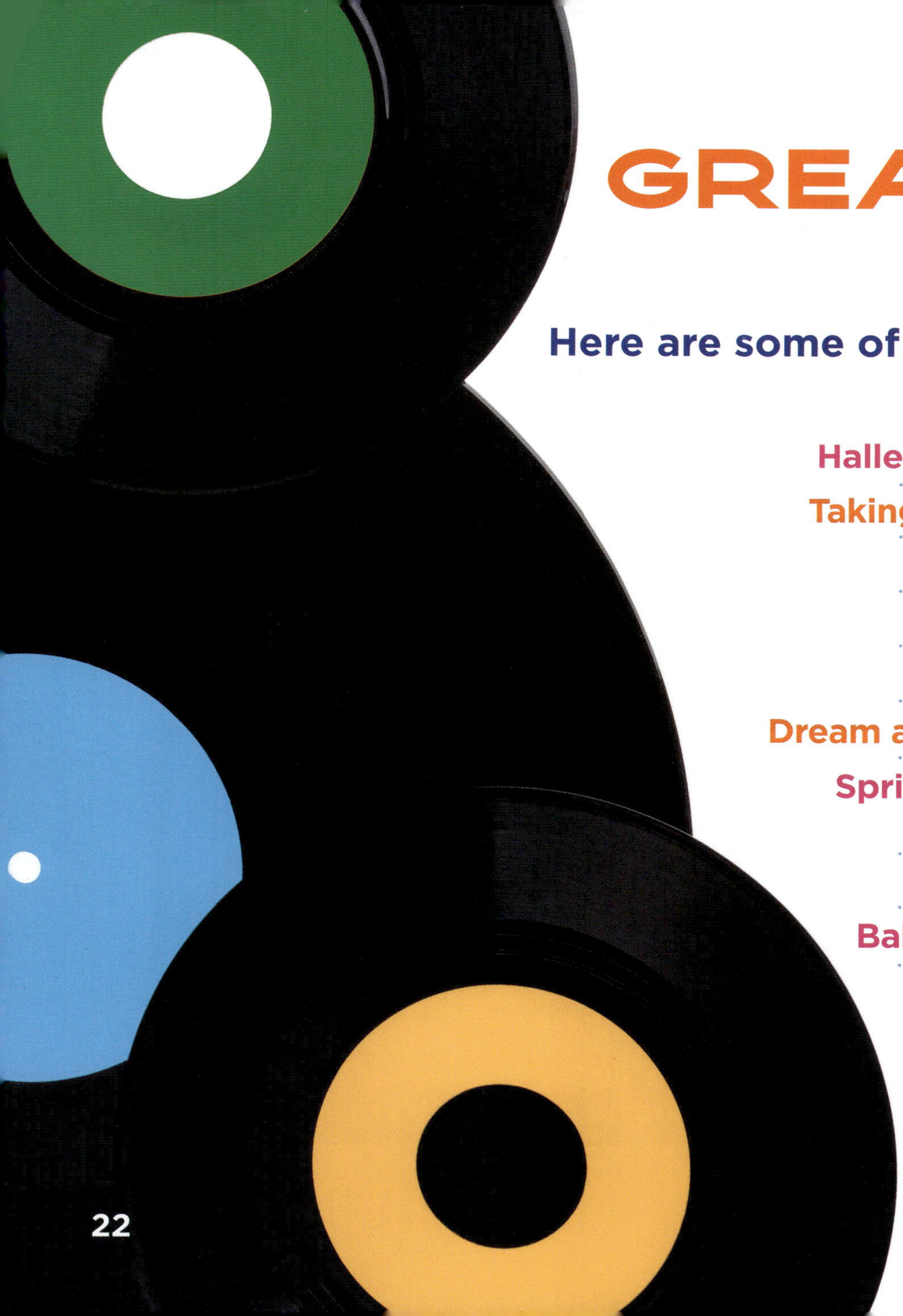

GREATEST HITS

Here are some of Ella Fitzgerald's signature songs:

Hallelujah, I Love Him So

Taking a Chance On Love

Mack the Knife

Over the Rainbow

Cheek to Cheek

Dream a Little Dream of Me

Spring Can Really Hang You Up the Most

A-Tisket, A-Tasket

Baby It's Cold Outside

Cry Me a River

Ella was the first African American woman to win a Grammy Award—and won 13 in all! She also won many other awards, including the **NAACP** Equal Justice Award.

ELLA'S IMPACT

In the 1970s, Ella started having health problems. She had heart surgery in 1986. But Ella kept performing. Her joyful voice continued to bring people together. And she quietly fought for equal rights for Black people.

In the 1990s, Ella's health worsened. She then spent a lot of time with her son and granddaughter, Alice. "I just want to smell the air, listen to the birds, and hear Alice laugh," said Ella. On June 15, 1996, Ella Fitzgerald died. The world **mourned** the loss of one of the greatest singers the world had ever known.

> "MAYBE I CAN SING IT AND YOU'LL UNDERSTAND."
> —ELLA FITZGERALD

Despite her fame, Ella faced **racism** throughout her life. Once, she was not allowed on an airplane because of her skin color. Another time, she and her bandmates were arrested in Texas for what the police said was gambling. The police were trying to stop Ella from performing. And when she got to the police station, the police "had the nerve to ask for an **autograph**," she said. Still, Ella held her head high and sang from her heart.

Ella had many famous friends, including Duke Ellington, Billie Holiday, Sarah Vaughan, and Marilyn Monroe (left). When Ella wasn't invited to sing in a nightclub because of the way she looked, Marilyn spoke up.

"WHERE THERE IS LOVE AND INSPIRATION, I DON'T THINK YOU CAN GO WRONG."
—ELLA FITZGERALD

Ella led the new band until 1942. She then became a solo performer, touring the world. Ella shared the stage with Louis Armstrong, Duke Ellington, and other greats. At the same time, she kept making albums. In the 1950s, Ella recorded more than 250 songs by other musicians. "It was a turning point in my life," she said.

In 1946, Ella fell in love with bass player Ray Brown (back right). They married and adopted a son. The marriage didn't last. But Ella and Ray stayed friends.

Norman Granz was an important jazz **producer** who became Ella's manager. Together, Norman and Ella chose songs that highlighted her voice. He helped boost Ella's career.

At age 21, Ella recorded "A-Tisket, A-Tasket." The song shot up the charts. Her recording sold 1 million copies! Ella was a star. Not long after, Chick Webb died. Ella took over the hard job of leading his band. At the time, this was a huge **feat** for a Black woman.

Pictured is bandleader and drummer Chick Webb.

The song "A-Tisket, A-Tasket" is based on a nursery rhyme. Ella turned it into a jazz song!

In 1936, Ella made her first of many records. She started singing bebop, a type of jazz. She used her voice to sound like the horns in the band. Ella featured this new sound, called scat, in the song "You'll Have to Swing It (Mr. Paganini)." Both Black and white fans were thrilled by Ella's groundbreaking scat singing.

Other songs that featured Ella's scat singing included "Flying Home" and "How High the Moon."

Ella met musician Benny Carter at the Apollo. Impressed with her talent, Benny also helped launch Ella's singing career. And they became lifelong friends.

MAKING MUSIC

After her big win at the Apollo, Ella sang wherever she could. In 1935, Ella won the chance to perform with the Tiny Bradshaw Band in Harlem. There she met drummer and bandleader Chick Webb. Chick already had a singer for his band. But he saw a "diamond in the rough" in Ella. So, Chick agreed to let Ella sing with his band at a college dance. He said, "If the kids like her, she stays." The students went wild for Ella. And Chick hired her on the spot.

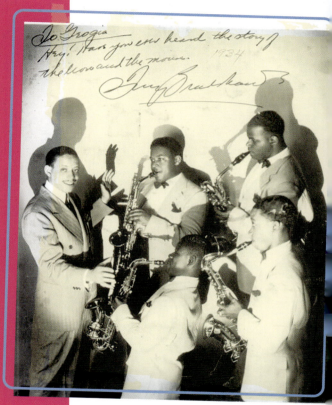

The Tiny Bradshaw Band in 1934

"THE ONLY THING BETTER THAN SINGING IS MORE SINGING."
—ELLA FITZGERALD

Ella grew to love being on stage.

In 1934, Ella entered an **amateur** contest at the Apollo Theater. Her friends dared her. She planned to dance but got nervous and sang instead. With Connee Boswell's voice in mind, Ella sang her heart out. And she won first prize! "Once up there, I felt the acceptance and love from the audience," Ella said. "I knew I wanted to sing before people the rest of my life."

Ella struggled after her mom died. She skipped school and got in trouble. Ella was sent to a **reform school** where things got even worse. She ran away but had no place to live. Then Ella's luck changed in a big way.

"JUST DON'T GIVE UP TRYING TO DO WHAT YOU REALLY WANT TO DO."
—ELLA FITZGERALD

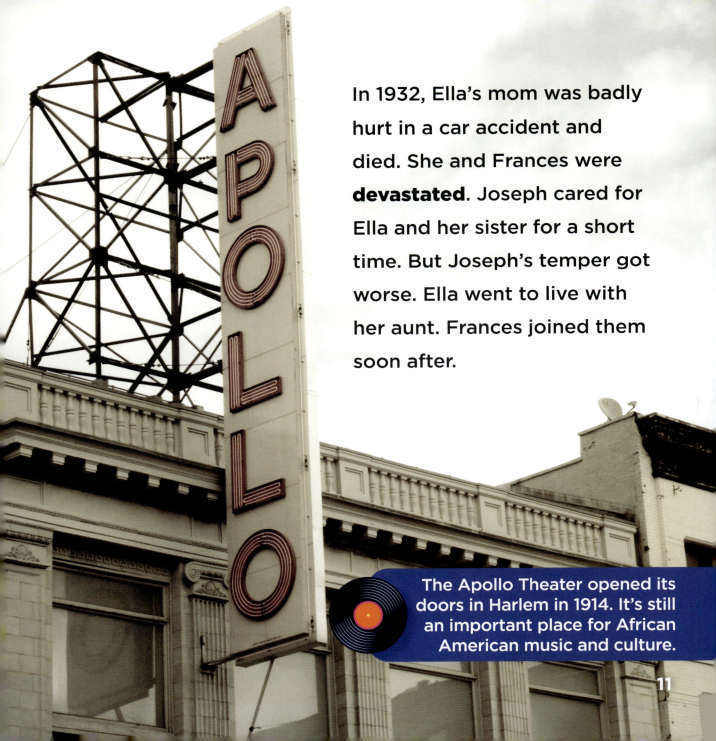

In 1932, Ella's mom was badly hurt in a car accident and died. She and Frances were **devastated**. Joseph cared for Ella and her sister for a short time. But Joseph's temper got worse. Ella went to live with her aunt. Frances joined them soon after.

The Apollo Theater opened its doors in Harlem in 1914. It's still an important place for African American music and culture.

Dancer Earl "Snakehips" Tucker was another of Ella's favorites. He wriggled his body like a snake. Young Ella learned his moves and danced on the bus and at school. Some evenings, she and her friends would take a train to Harlem, New York, to see performers at the Apollo Theater.

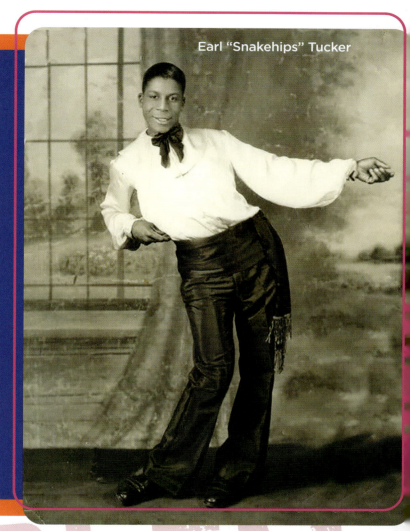

Earl "Snakehips" Tucker

Connee Boswell was Ella's favorite. "My mother brought home one of her records, and I fell in love with it," Ella said. She sang along to Connee's sweet voice, "*I've got the words, I've got the tune, I've been rehearsin' under the moon!*"

The Boswell Sisters

The Boswell Sisters were a singing trio from New Orleans, Louisiana. They were known for blending styles from Black and white musicians.

Both of Ella's parents were strict, and Joseph had a bad temper. So Ella spent a lot of time outside. When she wasn't playing baseball or other sports, Ella loved singing and dancing. She listened to jazz musicians, including Louis Armstrong and the Boswell Sisters.

The great jazz trumpeter and singer Louis Armstrong

"I SING LIKE I FEEL."
—ELLA FITZGERALD

Yonkers, New York

Ella and her family lived in a poor Italian neighborhood in Yonkers.

EARLY LIFE

Ella Jane Fitzgerald was born on April 25, 1917, in Newport News, Virginia. Her mother, Tempie, and father, William, separated soon after she was born. In the early 1920s, Ella and her mom moved to Yonkers, New York. They lived with Tempie's Portuguese boyfriend, Joseph. Tempie gave birth to Ella's half sister, Frances, in 1923. Joseph dug ditches and worked as a **chauffeur** to support his new family. Tempie worked in a **laundromat**.

As a young girl, Ella did well in school. In a report card, one of her teachers said she had musical talent and ambition.

Ella Fitzgerald was also called the "Queen of Jazz" and "Lady Ella."

THIS IS ELLA

Groundbreaking jazz singer Ella Fitzgerald is often called the "First Lady of Song." Known for her **vocal** range and **precision**, Ella moved people with her clear, joyful voice. During her 6-decade career, she achieved worldwide fame. Ella won 14 Grammy Awards and sold over 40 million albums. Her most important success, though, may be uniting people from different backgrounds with her music.

> "IT ISN'T WHERE YOU CAME FROM, IT'S WHERE YOU'RE GOING THAT COUNTS."
> —ELLA FITZGERALD

CONTENTS

This Is Ella 4
Early Life 6
Making Music 14
Ella's Impact 20

Greatest Hits 22
Glossary 23
Find Out More 24
Index 24
About the Author 24

Published in the United States of America by Cherry Lake Publishing
Ann Arbor, Michigan
www.cherrylakepublishing.com

Reading Adviser: Beth Walker Gambro, MS, Ed., Reading Consultant, Yorkville, IL
Content Adviser: Michael Kramer, PhD, Music Historian
Book Designer: Ed Morgan

Photo Credits: © Everett Collection Inc/Alamy Stock Photo, cover and title page; Library of Congress/William P. Gottleib Jazz Photos, 5; Wikimedia Commons/Carl Van Vechten, 6; © Tango Images/Alamy Stock Photo, 7; Wikimedia Commons, 8; Wikimedia Commons, 9; Wikimedia Commons, 10; flickr/Julien Chatelain, 11; © Pictorial Press Ltd/Alamy Stock Photo, 12; Wikimedia Commons, 13; Courtesy of The State Archives of Florida, 14; Wikimedia Commons, 15 top; Library of Congress/William P. Gottleib Jazz Photos, 15 bottom; © Phillipe Gras/Alamy Stock Photo, 16; © Pictorial Press Ltd/Alamy Stock Photo, 17; Library of Congress/William P. Gottleib Jazz Photos, 18; Wikimedia Commons, 19 left; © Allstar Picture Library Limited/Alamy Stock Photo, 19 right; Wikimedia Commons/Olavi Kaskisuo/Lehtikuva, 21; freepik.com, 22.

Copyright © 2024 by Cherry Lake Publishing Group

All rights reserved. No part of this book may be reproduced or utilized in any form or by any means without written permission from the publisher.

Cherry Lake Press is an imprint of Cherry Lake Publishing Group.

Library of Congress Cataloging-in-Publication Data

Names: Markovics, Joyce L., author.
Title: Ella Fitzgerald / by Joyce Markovics.
Description: Ann Arbor, Michigan : Cherry Lake Publishing, 2023. | Series: Groundbreakers: Black musicians | Includes bibliographical references and index. | Audience: Grades 4-6
Identifiers: LCCN 2023003454 (print) | LCCN 2023003455 (ebook) | ISBN 9781668927816 (hardcover) | ISBN 9781668928868 (paperback) | ISBN 9781668930335 (epub) | ISBN 9781668931813 (pdf) | ISBN 9781668933299 (kindle edition) | ISBN 9781668934777 (ebook)
Subjects: LCSH: Fitzgerald, Ella—Juvenile literature. | Jazz musicians—United States—Biography—Juvenile literature. | Singers—United States—Biography—Juvenile literature.
Classification: LCC ML3930.F5 M37 2023 (print) | LCC ML3930.F5 (ebook) | DDC 782.42165092 [B]—dc23/eng/20230125
LC record available at https://lccn.loc.gov/2023003454
LC ebook record available at https://lccn.loc.gov/2023003455

Printed in the United States of America by
Corporate Graphics

Note from publisher: Websites change regularly, and their future contents are outside of our control. Supervise children when conducting any recommended online searches for extended learning opportunities.